Walking through Advent

Walking through Advent

Daily readings

Jan Sutch Pickard

wild goose
publications

www.ionabooks.com

© 2014 Jan Sutch Pickard

First published 2014 by
Wild Goose Publications, Fourth Floor, Savoy House,
140 Sauchiehall Street, Glasgow G2 3DH, UK,
the publishing division of the Iona Community.
Scottish Charity No. SC003794. Limited Company Reg. No. SC096243.

ISBN 978-1-84952-311-0

Cover calligraphy © Stephen Raw | www.stephenraw.com
Cover background image © Midosemsem | Dreamstime.com

Overseas distribution
Australia: Willow Connection Pty Ltd, Unit 4A, 3–9 Kenneth Road,
Manly Vale, NSW 2093
New Zealand: Pleroma, Higginson Street, Otane 4170, Central Hawkes Bay
Canada: Bayard Distribution, 10 Lower Spadina Ave., Suite 400, Toronto,
Ontario M5V 2Z

Printed by Bell & Bain, Thornliebank, Glasgow

Contents

TO LOVE MERCY
ACT JUSTLY
and WALK
HUMBLY
WITH YOUR GOD

Introduction

What does the Lord ask of you?
To love mercy, act justly
and walk humbly with your God. (Micah 6:8)

Advent is a time of wonder and waiting. Wonder at the mystery of Incarnation: the Maker of the universe born as a helpless child. Wondering what on earth God is going to do next. And – in this time of expectancy – reflecting on what is expected of us, as God's family. Advent is a time of waiting – but that's not a passive thing. We need to walk into Advent with our eyes open.

We walk through wintery weather, festive preparations, stressful busyness, expectations that can't easily be met: common experiences, these. We walk through memories of other Decembers, of happy and hard times with our own families. We walk through whatever is happening in the communities of which we are part – whether that's conflict or celebration. We walk through a world where wars are being waged and babies are being born. We are humbled by our inability to do much about what is wrong. But we do our best: to be kind, caring, to understand the meaning of mercy. We do our best to be even-handed, to act justly. We are helped in this by walking with other people, friends and strangers – we learn from them. Most of all we are helped by the knowledge that God walks with us.

That is why this book is called *Walking through Advent.*

Some of the daily reflections here came into my mind while I walked along the roads or the shoreline of the Isle of Mull, where I live. Others were inspired by watching people on pilgrimage, arriving in Iona. In the course of writing this, I spent time with friends whose great delight is to cover wilderness miles – *stravaiging* – and others for whom taking even a few steps across a room is an achievement. They share this Advent journey. So do men and women I met when I set my feet on the ground in Palestine. I was serving as an Ecumenical Accompanier in a World Council of Churches programme (www.eappi.org) which supports the presence of international peace observers in a situation of conflict – where Palestinians in the land that we call 'holy' live under occupation. God is there too and in other conflict situations – 'God-with-us' – a guide, protector and companion on the road.

Sometimes (wherever you are) it is hard going – and sometimes there are bursts of sunlight and moments of joy. To remind me of what's really important I have the words from Micah on the wall in my home. But it's another quotation, from George Fox (below), painted in dancing callig-raphy, that's the first thing I see when I wake each morning. Valuing soli-tude, and the reflection to which we're called in Advent, I know too that encounters with other people – different from me and each unique and precious in the eyes of God – can be surprising, challenging, sustaining. To live this way is a blessing:

'Walk cheerfully over the world, answering that of God in everyone.'

November 27: You trace my journeying

Lord, you have examined me and you know me.
You know me at rest and in action;
you discern my thoughts from afar.
You trace my journeying and my resting places,
and are familiar with all the paths I take … (Psalm 139:1–4)

Read the whole of Psalm 139.

Reflect on God's deep knowledge of us, our actions and our thoughts:

It encompasses us – inescapable, and also protective.

From our beginnings in the womb – in our DNA – shaping us and determining much that happens in our lives.

We have free will, and can make wrong choices; yet Christians believe that God's love is unconditional. It is a mystery that is beyond us. Yet it contains us.

The outburst of anger and hatred in verses 19-22 is an example of the way that the psalms reflect human nature, human brokenness. God, who *'discerns our thoughts from afar'*, knows that we aren't always tolerant or generous in spirit.

The psalm ends with a plea: *know my mind … understand my anxious thoughts.*

Blessing

May God, who is present in sunrise and nightfall,
and in the crossing of the sea,
guide your feet as you go.
May God, who is with you
when you sit and when you stand,
encompass you with love
and lead you by the hand.

May God, who knows your path
and the places where you rest,
be with you in your waiting,
be your good news for sharing,
and lead you in the way that is everlasting. Amen

November 28: Flying with crutches

We were like people renewed in health.
Our mouths were full of laughter
and our tongues sang aloud for joy. (Psalm 126:1,2a)

This psalm reminds me of the story in Acts 3 of the man who, begging at the Beautiful Gate in Jerusalem, was healed by Peter, who said, 'I have no silver or gold; but what I have I give you: in the name of Jesus Christ of Nazareth, get up and walk.' The story goes on: 'Then, grasping him by the right hand, he helped the man up; and at once his feet and ankles grew strong; he sprang to his feet and started to walk. He entered the Temple with them, leaping and praising God as he went. Everyone saw him walking and praising God and … they were filled with wonder …'

This story is about the coming-into-being of the early Church. Peter and John are seen as apprentice apostles, discovering the power to heal, finding words to declare their faith, seeing the meaning of resurrection demonstrated in people's lives.

The psalm also reminds me of a friend, whose story of healing is not about cure but about courage and God's transforming power.

Patricia, registered blind, took time to recover from a broken leg. I wondered, did her vigorous enquiring mind and sense of humour compensate for also spending time in a wheelchair – or increase the frustration? The way she described her experience opened my eyes:

Flying with crutches

I am airborne! Promoted from a sturdy Zimmer frame
to the rampant rolling gait of crutches.
Nonchalantly concealing inordinate effort,
I stroll the corridors and climb the stairs of rehabilitation.
When you have been helpless for many weeks,
to be pushed month after month in wheelchairs,
dependent on the will of others for all your coming and going –
mobility becomes a word with new meaning.
Like a pushy thrush, straining to the nest's rim,
I am airborne even before I fly.

(Patricia Smith)

God, help us to understand what healing means for each of us,
so that in spirit we may leap up, laugh for joy, praise you, learn to fly.

November 29: God who walks with us

Jesus said to them: 'Come, follow me.' (Mark 1:17)

First there was a call
to us, in the midst of daily life,
to set out on a journey – not escaping –
challenged to live otherwise in the world:
'Follow me.'

At the roadside,
in the marketplace, on doorsteps,
in the gutter – encounters
which changed us for ever:
'Do you want to be healed?'

Along the way,
conversations which were not easy –
questioning our assumptions,
threatening our status:
'The first shall be last and the last first.'

Resting on hillsides and in homes,
sharing food for the journey,
friendship, stories, laughter –
being known in the breaking of bread:
'This is my body … you are my body.'

Weeping for the city,
whose stones cry out against injustice,

walking its streets, carrying the world's pain
to the place of execution:
'You must take up your cross.'

Running from the tomb,
scarcely believing our eyes –
full of the good news,
challenged to travel on:
'Go and tell my brothers ... Go into all the world.'

God, who walks with us,
give us imagination, courage, grace
to be companions of the Way. Amen

November 30: A child, bringing bread

With justice he will judge the poor
and defend the humble in the land with equity …
The calf and the young lion will feed together,
and a little child shall lead them. (Isaiah 11:6)

The children walk slowly, carefully down the length of the Abbey, from sunlight through shadow, over the ancient flagstones. In their hands they are carrying bread, to give to the waiting people. This Sunday morning in Iona, the congregation's a real mixture: holidaymakers staying at different places on the island, islanders who will also go on to the Parish Church, Iona Community staff and volunteers of different ages and nationalities, and the guests who are staying in the Abbey and MacLeod Centre. This week, the Centres are full of people from urban priority areas. Some of them bear the marks of a life of deprivation or coping on the edges of an unequal society.

There are people in their Sunday best, and some with startling tattoos, folk who have been out of work for years, men who have struggled with dependency on alcohol or drugs, grandmothers who are the main carers for lively little ones, asylum seekers needing sanctuary from places of conflict: human beings with a great variety of life experience, united by this journey they've made, the shared experience of this moment.

The sermon is a challenging story about justice; the songs make all our hearts dance (the children dance too). Then, with words that are both earthy and uplifting, we come to Communion, or rather it comes to us. Representatives of this mix of humanity walk through the congregation, carrying the bread and wine. A child so small she could barely peep over the Table is now accompanied by her grandmother – but is trusted to carry the bread. The cup offered to me comes from the hands of a young boy from Sri Lanka, his father watching over him. From their vulnerability to ours, the gift of bread and wine – broken bread in a community which knows about brokenness. What happens for all of us is a moment of wholeness, hope.

Welcome to this ancient place:
house of prayer for many nations; home to all who come.
Welcome to this gathering place:
friend and stranger, saint and sinner, in all who gather here.
Come with hope or hesitation; come with joy or yearning;
all who hunger, all who thirst for life in all its fullness.
Generous God and generous Saviour, touch us through your Spirit.

(Responses from the Sunday morning service in Iona Abbey)

December 1: The Visitation

Soon afterwards Mary set out and hurried away to a town in the uplands of Judah. She went into Zechariah's house and greeted Elizabeth. And when Elizabeth heard Mary's greeting, the baby stirred in her womb. Then Elizabeth was filled with the Holy Spirit and exclaimed in a loud voice, 'God's blessing is on you above all women and his blessing is on the fruit of your womb. Who am I that the mother of my Lord should visit me? I tell you, when your greeting sounded in my ears, the baby in my womb leapt for joy.' (Luke 1:39–44)

Mary, learning of her pregnancy, filled with the wonder of carrying God's child, hurried to find someone in whom she could confide. Her much older cousin Elizabeth lived in the hills outside Jerusalem – a long journey from Nazareth for a young woman in the first trimester. Elizabeth was also expecting a baby – who would become John the Baptist.

Artists through the ages have tried to capture the intimacy and joy of this encounter between the two women. American artist Bill Viola works in photography and video. His installations have surprising spiritual power, combining the beauty of human beings doing down-to-earth things, with a sense of mystery. On YouTube there is a very short video of his called *The Greeting*. A tall young woman in a vivid red dress and sandals moves with swift steps toward an older woman, who is waiting for her. They stretch out arms to each other; they embrace.

The home of Elizabeth and her husband Zechariah (that is, the place traditionally associated with the birth of John the Baptist) is called Ein Kerem or Karem. It is just a few kilometres from the city of Jerusalem. Wooded hillsides rise above a village which was depopulated on the founding of the State of Israel in 1948. Unlike Deir Yassin, just two kilometres away, there was no massacre there, but the Palestinian population was evacuated. The old houses were not demolished but reoccupied by Jewish families, many of them artists. It is now a popular place for tourists and pilgrims to visit.

Christian pilgrims may pause at the Church of the Visitation, to recite the Magnificat – Mary's response to Elizabeth's greeting. Or they fill bottles with water believed to be holy, from the ancient spring welling up under an arch in the centre of the village – tradition says that the two women met here.

Waiting God, where will we find you?
Encouraged by your Spirit, hurrying, searching,
we meet you in other people.
Not knowing what the future will bring, may we continue on our journeys
surprised by joy, refreshed by your living water. Amen

December 2: Pink knitting

'You knitted me together in my mother's womb. I praise you, for you fill me with awe; wonderful you are and wonderful your works. You know me through and through. (Psalm 139:13)

References to knitting in the Bible are few! I'm not a biblical scholar, but I'm sure of that. My knitting is pretty basic too. My mother, on the other hand, produced beautiful garments for us as children, and then for her grandchildren – jerseys and gloves and tam-o'-shanters. She began learning Fair Isle patterns while staying with my father on that island (where I was conceived). She remembered women walking the island tracks and knitting as they went – and regretted that she never achieved that skill.

When I reached the age when she put her needles aside, I took mine up, as part of the project Wool Against Weapons. This year the Campaign for Nuclear Disarmament encouraged people to knit or crochet lengths 60 cm wide and 100 cm long, in predominately pink yarn. These were joined together and the communal creation had its first outing at a demonstration on the Royal Mile in Edinburgh. Then on 9 August (Nagasaki Day) 2014, with much more added, it was unrolled on the road between Burghfield and Aldermaston, to stretch for seven miles and make a strong (and colourful) point about opposition to the weapons of mass destruction produced there. By contrast knitting is a creative – and very peaceful – activity.

In the preceding months, I had the opportunity to be where knitting was happening – in people's kitchens, on a train, in a café, with veteran peace activists Helen and Ellen, with absolute beginners, in the MacLeod Centre craft room, where I wrote:

Pink wool – everywhere –
dancing needles, strands of hope,
hands busy for peace.

By now the long scarf will have been unpicked and sewn into blankets for people who would otherwise be cold this winter. All this year, knitting companionably, people have been sharing with each other family news and discussing peace issues: weaving their lives, their personal hopes and fears for the world, into that foolish, inspired creation.

Creator God
you know us through and through:
you know what we fear, and what we hold most dear.
Where war is taken for granted, help us to make a stand:
making peace, while making things with our hands. Amen

December 3: On pilgrimage

I rejoiced when they said to me, 'Let us go to the house of the Lord'. Now we are standing within your gates … pray for the peace of Jerusalem: may those who love you prosper; peace be within your ramparts and prosperity in your palaces. For the sake of these my brothers and my friends, I shall say 'Peace be within you.' (Psalm 122:1,2,6–8)

What a mixture! The crowds who travelled to Jerusalem for festivals in Jesus' time: everyone on foot, some travelling light; some bringing cooking pots and bed-rolls; some rich enough to have a donkey to carry their baggage, so you'd hear braying among the praying; some with pigeons or sheep to sacrifice, so there would be cooing and bleating and the smell of dung; serious pilgrims focused on their destination; large and cheerful family groups, where a twelve-year-old boy could get safely lost in the crowd for days on end; small children jumping up and down at the first view of the city; pilgrim songs being started by one group and picked up by those further down the line. This would have been part of the pattern of Mary and Joseph's life, long before she travelled to see Elizabeth, before they went to Bethlehem for the census – they would have been on pilgrimage to Jerusalem. A long journey, a chosen journey full of meaning.

What a mixture! The folk coming off the Iona ferry: happy holidaymakers and tired travellers. Folk with rucksacks and roll-along suitcases. Some are stepping once again on familiar and well-loved ground. For others everything is new – crossing Mull, crossing the sea, seeing white beaches, green meadows, a little mountain, a big church. A small island – yet a place pregnant with possibilities. There are men with golf clubs, women with easels, children with surfboards, backpackers with guitars – each has high expectations. And there are pilgrims, in groups or on their own. They have come a long way for this, expecting to find God – or themselves.

Some people place a halo round Iona, responding to the idea of 'a thin place'. Is this holy ground or just a down-to-earth Hebridean island, or both? What makes it special is what people – pilgrims – bring to it, not their roll-along suitcases, but the richness of the rest of their lives, their stories, their gifts and creativity, their willingness to take risks and enter into community, their hopes, their prayers.

Bless to us, O God,
the earth beneath our feet.
Bless to us, O God,
the path whereon we go.
Bless to us, O God,
the people whom we meet.

(Prayer from the Gaelic, used in the weekly pilgrimage round Iona)

December 4: 'Yes, I sing to my sheep'

Like a shepherd he will tend his flock and with his arms keep them together; he will carry the lambs in his bosom and lead the ewes to water. (Isaiah 40:11)

High in the mountains overlooking the Jordan Valley is a small Palestinian village. For generations farming families have cared for their sheep and olive and almond trees, growing small crops of wheat, chickpeas – subsistence farming. But on the hilltops Israeli settlement outposts include huge barns – factory farming on stolen land. The 'security zone' around these buildings stretches down the hillside toward the village. Armed settlers turn back the shepherds trying to find grazing for their flocks. Where once they had roamed over the hills and all the way down to the Jordan, now they have access to less and less land. The custom is for the shepherds to stay with their flocks all day – now, as well as packs of wild dogs, there is danger from settlers who shoot to kill the sheep or maim them, or attack the shepherds themselves.

I witnessed the life of this community when I lived in the village for several months as part of a 'non-violent presence', with the Ecumenical Accompaniment Programme in Palestine and Israel.

I saw Kemal leading his flock along a limestone edge, as high as he dare go on the hillside. As they moved slowly through the scrub, he sang to them, a beautiful plaintive melody, echoing from the rocks. Later I met him as he brought the sheep home. 'Kemal, do you always sing to your sheep?' Standing waist-deep in his flock, he smiled at me, as though I was asking a daft question. 'Yes, I sing to my sheep. They know my voice, and when I sing they follow me, not go into danger, find grass. The goats too – they are gentle, and they come with me – when I sing.'

*God, thank you for what we can learn – from a working man
in a hard place, in difficult times – about your steadfast love and care:
thank you for leading us, calming us, keeping us safe, and feeding us
through the stories and the lives of our brothers and sisters. Amen*

December 5: Learning to walk again

'The people who walked in darkness have seen a great light;
on those who lived in a land as dark as death a light has dawned.
You have increased their joy and given them great gladness. (Isaiah 9:2,3a)

It wasn't quite a land as dark as death, but my mobility had diminished and pain had increased over the previous year. I was losing the enthusiasm, and confidence, to do necessary things, never mind new ones – initiatives, adventures. So I agreed to an operation to replace both my knees, which meant putting myself into the hands of other people, and the 'little death' of a general anaesthetic. Then I undertook the long process of recuperation. And it turned out to be a very good experience – though painful at first, and humiliating at times. But I found myself giving thanks for the skill of doctors, nurses, physiotherapists. And I *found myself* in other ways too, as, day by day, I did the prescribed exercises – and walked, carefully, mindfully, a few steps further; starting in the dark of late-autumn mornings; stopping to watch the lightening sky, feeling the hope of each new day, while marvelling at this journey of renewed health – and of course watching where I put my feet.

Walking Advent

Walking in darkness
feet feeling the way –
while light like an incoming tide
flows between the clouds
slowly opening the sky
transforming the earth –
my feet on the ground,

each sole feeling the difference
of turf, stone, mud;
learning to walk again,
plodding painfully,
looking foolish
human, humble;
walking slowly, mindfully,
aware of my own mortal body
and other little lives
in this turning world:
aware of the huge pain
of hurricanes, homelessness,
of hunger and anger;
but going on, steadily walking
and looking for the dawn –
walking humbly with God.

December 6: On the shore

If I travel to the limits of the east or dwell at the bounds of the western sea, even there your hand will be guiding me, your right hand holding me fast. (Psalm 139:9,10)

I spend much of my time reading and writing. The discipline of housework is neglected because of this, though such things are also a discipline – and a source of great delight. But I need to care for my body as well as my mind – and so each day, whatever the weather, I walk for an hour or more. Because I live on an island, I will often be walking beside the sea.

Walk by its side

The sea breathes more slowly than you or I –
three human breaths for every shore-long sigh –
we watch it busy with the task in hand,
bringing in kelp to strew along the sand;
rubbing out bird-prints and footprints,
messiness and messages,
our moments of fame, our names:
the sea teaches us that nothing stays the same.
With every wave, with each tide,
it's rearranging, it's changing,
beach-cleaning and finding new meaning.

So come with me, accompany the sea,
learn from it, walk by its side.

God, our Creator and our Carer,
wherever we live, and wherever we wander,
we are never far from you.
Help us to learn from your creation
about your power for change.
And help me to know, as you walk with me,
how you cherish me, just as I am. Amen

December 7: At the Bethlehem checkpoint

In the tender compassion of our God
the dawn from heaven will break upon us,
to shine on those who live in darkness, under the shadow of death,
and to guide our feet into the way of peace. (Luke 1:78–79)

Early in the morning, Ecumenical Accompaniers from the Bethlehem team get up and walk to Checkpoint 300, between that Palestinian city and Jerusalem. While there is a big gate in the Separation Barrier for tourist coaches, people on foot – trying to leave Bethlehem for hospital or family visits, for study or work – need to queue at a different point, in a long structure like a cattle crush, to get to a turnstile and the first of several ID and security controls. Those who are fortunate enough to have jobs in Jerusalem need to start queuing at 3 or 4 am, in order to be at work in time – if they are not turned back by the soldiers.

Just breathing

Dark and cold before dawn, where men
who rose much earlier, are waiting to go to work,
packed into long narrow pens that run
the length of the ramp, along that concrete wall,
scrawled with scorn and defiance: though in the dark
no-one can see the writing on the wall;
nor can you see the faces of these men
huddled together, leaning on the wire fence
which bulges with the weight of humanity
barely contained; all you can see is – here a hand
grasping a bar – there, breath puffed out in the chill air;

or spidering forms against the sky, trying to climb
into a cage already crammed, through razor wire;
weary with standing still for more than an hour,
a score of men are sitting down on the ground
by common consent, shoulder to shoulder,
their upturned faces catching what light there is;
here someone coughs … over there
a man lights a cigarette and passes it round;
no-one is talking – what is there to say?
Yet, filling the dark, a shapeless sound like grieving:
seven hundred men waiting for someone to open a gate,
hoping for a way out, and just breathing.

Prayer

Breathe, and be aware of your breathing.
Breathe out: the inhumanity of the Separation Barrier and checkpoint;
breathe in: God is present in this place too. Pray for change.

December 8: Beautiful feet

How beautiful on the mountains are the feet of the herald,
the bringer of good news, announcing salvation.(Isaiah 52:7)

This is a poem I wrote for Warren, a friend celebrating 50 years of ordained – and very varied – ministry, which for me is a reminder of the ministry to which we are all called.

Are your feet beautiful, Warren?

Are your feet beautiful? What a personal question! But relevant.
Your feet must be worn by now: not worn-out but well-used.
You've trodden stony tracks, bush paths, city streets,
mountain heights and dark valleys, pilgrim ways –
your whole life has been a journey.

These feet have carried the word of the Gospel
to African villages and Black Country chapels;
have paced the flagstones of the Abbey Church –
where work, worship and walking belong together –
joining the complex dance of community;
these feet faithfully journeyed with a life-companion, Joan;
they keep pace with friends, sometimes they walk alone.

Larks were exulting, wild geese calling,
as you trod the muddy moorland track to Camas.
These feet have carried you, early in the morning,
to the grim Separation Barrier in Bethlehem,
witnessing at the checkpoint,

accompanying oppressed and courageous people;
standing your ground on God's *kairos*.
Worn, wounded, dirty with being down-to-earth –
are your feet beautiful?
These are the feet of one who brings good news, the feet of a disciple.
Jesus knelt to wash them. They are beautiful.

God of journeys, God who is the good news we share,
bless our well-worn but beautiful feet! Amen

December 9: Travels with a donkey

Joseph went up to Judaea from the town of Nazareth in Galilee, to register in the city of David called Bethlehem … and with him went Mary, his betrothed, who was expecting her child.' (Luke 2:4,5)

Have your Christmas cards started to arrive? Almost certainly some will show the couple making their way to Bethlehem, Joseph plodding on the long road, leading Mary on a donkey. But wait a minute, where is that donkey in the Bible? It's not mentioned in Luke's brief account of the reason for their journey. Again, we guess that the manger, where Mary laid the newborn child, was in a stable – a natural place to find a donkey – but, unlike the Christmas cards, Luke's Gospel overlooks this detail. And when Matthew's Gospel tells us about Joseph being warned in a dream about Herod, taking mother and child by night and seeking refuge for them in Egypt – where's the donkey? Only on the cards.

Trotting through the stories we have been told since childhood, is this little donkey, this friendly, hard-working, long-suffering and completely fictional detail. It comes between us and a story of an occupying power, displaced people, temporary shelter, threats of death, last-minute flight. A story as terrifying as those in the news as I write this: Syria, Sudan, the Central African Republic, Gaza. The radio news this morning mentioned Palestinians fleeing the Israeli bombardment to places of safety in UN compounds 'in their donkey carts'. Imagining that scene of terror, I remembered one of low-level anxiety: I stood at a checkpoint as Palestinian farmers from the little town of Jayyous tried to access their land behind the Separation Barrier. I saw the donkeys with carts waiting long in the hot sun, subjected to searches at gunpoint like their owners. The

Arab word for the human quality of waiting patiently, long-suffering, endurance is *sumoud*.

Perhaps the value of the donkeys on our Christmas cards is not to distract us from the harsh realities of the Incarnation, but to remind us that this story is about God present in our common humanity, close to the suffering of earth's creatures, God found in something as down to earth as *sumoud*.

God of creatures great and small,
we thank you for those that accompany us on our journey through life,
and belong in the stories that we tell,
and for all we can learn from them – patience, usefulness, and trust. Amen

December 10: At the roadside

Yea, though I walk in death's dark vale,
Yet will I fear none ill:
For thou art with me; and thy rod
And staff me comfort still. (Metrical version of Psalm 23)

The sound of a congregation singing to the well-loved tune 'Crimond' overflows from the little building by the loch. St Ernan's Kirk, Creich is packed with people. There are many more in the churchyard. Cars are parked for half a mile along the verge of the single-track road, so that tour buses have to creep past like caterpillars, with a row of faces staring in bemusement at the funeral crowd. But this doesn't look like death's dark vale. It is high summer. Men in Sunday best have taken off their jackets to show white shirts. Silent people seek the shade of stone walls, or sit down on the green grass. The midday sun sparkles on the loch: a scene of serene beauty – and community.

Folk have gathered to remember the life of Gerry, who for many years drove those tour buses, and the service buses which are a lifeline to local folk. As a driver on Mull he must have been familiar with every blind corner, right-angled bridge, passing place and pothole. He knew the road well and the destination of most of his passengers. 'And then one day,' he used to say, 'I decided to go and see what it was all about.' So he gave up his job on the buses and went to work as a guide for Historic Scotland in Iona. Bus drivers can be grumpy; now a different side of his nature was set free – his interest in history, his ability to relate to people, his creativity in making videos, his Glaswegian sense of humour. Like a caterpillar becoming a butterfly.

In silence, in the sunshine outside the church, by the side of his well-travelled road, we remembered this.

God-with-us, set us free
from ways of being that deny your life in us.
You know all the roads we travel –
may they bring us to where we can fulfil our calling –
until at last we find rest and rejoice in your presence. Amen

December 11: Zahra

Blessed are those who hunger and thirst to see right prevail. (Matthew 5:3–6)

It is just six-thirty in the morning, but it is already very hot and dry at the Farmer's Gate, below Jayyous, a village set on a hill in the West Bank. Every day its people look out across the Separation Barrier to their stolen farmland. And as the sun rises the farmers come to the gate, in the hope of being allowed through to work on their land. A donkey cart comes down the track and the driver stops just before the gate, lifts out of the cart a large plastic container and puts it down where the people on foot are queueing to show their ID to soldiers at the checkpoint. He greets us, the Ecumenical Accompaniers watching at the gate, then moves up to wait his turn.

A woman is following him down the road. She is old, but not bowed, walking slowly but with dignity. We've seen her on other days, going through the checkpoint, with her scarfed head held high, speaking to the soldiers briefly, with emphasis, a stern grandmother. We've greeted her, and she has told us her name – Zahra. She is a widow, the only person in her household with a permit to go to the family's olive grove. This morning she is carrying an empty sack, to harvest some of their olives. The other farmer had relieved her of the burden of the large container, for the first stage of her journey. We greet her and ask what it is; she shows us – it's full of water.

Why is she taking water to her orchard? This is the dry season, but there isn't nearly enough in it to irrigate her olive trees. We guess it might be water to quench her thirst in the heat of the day. We mime drinking – but she shakes her head. It is Ramadan. She's fasting – and that includes refraining from drinking for twelve daylight hours.

Then what is the water for? 'Praying,' she says, and mimes the ritual washing before prayer. That's why she's carrying water to the farmlands – so that she can pray properly, in the midst of her daily work.

Zahra picks up her water-pot, and walks towards the soldiers at the gate. In a land yearning for justice, a woman who hungers and thirsts to find God's way.

Just and merciful God,
may we learn from Zahra, in her sumoud, *her steadfastness,*
and bear witness to the injustice she meets in her daily life.
Give us grace to accompany her on her journey of faith;
may we know what it is to hunger and thirst for justice –
and may the yearning of all your people be satisfied. Amen

December 12: Feet on the ground

A voice cries: 'Clear a road through the wilderness for the Lord, prepare a highway across the desert for our God; let every valley be raised, every mountain and hill be brought low, uneven ground be made smooth, and steep places become level. Then will the glory of the Lord be revealed for all humankind to see.' (Isaiah 40:3–5)

Not a highway across the desert, but a track across the field, where some work had been done, that winter, to drain the land and improve the access. But what looked smooth was slick with mud – as I discovered when I stepped on – and into – it. The strong red clay clung to my boots; when I struggled, I lost them. I was laughing helplessly, as were other folk walking down to the shore on that New Year's Day. But I needed to get back for the afternoon service in the parish church. I arrived just in time, with most of the mud cleaned off, and with some new insights – that holy ground can be found anywhere; that the glory of God is seen in stars and in mud.

Feet on the ground (I)

It was red mud, red as Adam,
and it sucked the shoes right off my feet,
so I stood barefoot – or at least in holey socks –
on the cold and mucky ground.

It was New Year's Day
and I was trying to make my way back
to polite people in a chill church, with a story
about the heavens' glory and wise men following a star.

Now I was stopped in my tracks,
looking foolish and laughing helplessly
at this unexpected gift of having to get
my hands dirty, saving my shoes.

Sheep grazed, unimpressed,
clouds unfurled overhead, sudden light
struck the sea horizon – and then and there I found
more than my footwear.

The stars still sang in their courses,
while, in worship, the words that came to me
were down to earth:
since I'd stood on just-as-holy ground
with mud between my toes.

Down-to-earth God, thank you for experiences that humble us,
remind us of our humanity and make us laugh. Amen

December 13: Reflection in a garden

Restore our fortunes, Lord, as streams return in the Negeb.
Those who sow in tears will reap with songs of joy. (Psalm 126:4,5)

Stepping from slate to beaten earth – brushing aside the fern fronds – from a wooden walkway to cobbles, pausing, turning back; treading on grass, flagstones, stepping stones (or stumbling blocks), clinker, brick, playground rubber tiles; under a bower of trees, across gravel from a riverbed and yielding turf: a mindful walk within a small space.

Space and time opening up like a flower, within mind and soul.

I was visiting friends, John and Chris, fellow members of the Iona Community, who have created – over years of hard physical work – a reflective garden, themed according to Ignatian spirituality. Many words could be used to explain what each part of the garden is about. Words like Loving Creator, sin (and waste of the earth's resources) and repentance, hospitality, the call to discipleship (and the choices involved), passion, death and resurrection – with the possibilities of new life.

But beyond words was the physical sensation of walking through this garden, seeing sunlight dappling through hazel leaves; repelled by a riverbed of abandoned plastic bottles, reminding of the wasteful way we live in the world; blinking at the fierce reds of flowers around a wooden cross in the Passion garden, feeling jagged clinker underfoot; smelling fragrance of catmint and lavender, aware of running water, playing with a solar fountain which rises and falls, responding to a human hand moving like a cloud over the sun; hearing birdsong – and human voices from beyond the garden – stepping on cool damp grass in the labyrinth …

God of growing things, we thank you for gardens,
carved out, planted and nurtured by hard-working human hands;
we thank you for the great garden of creation in which we live,
and all that it teaches us about your love;
and we thank you for Jesus' feet walking this earth,
on rough and gentle paths – through tears to joy –
and for time and space for our own feet to follow. Amen

December 14: Justice and peace embrace

Love and faithfulness are companions: justice and peace embrace.
Faithfulness walks on the earth and justice looks down from heaven.
The children of God will flourish and the land will be fruitful.
Justice will be a sign of the coming Kingdom: the path to it will be peace.
(Psalm 85:10–13, paraphrase)

In Iona this summer I joined a small group of friends who had waited many years to make this pilgrimage together. Nigel and Jill had first come a few years ago, walking several hundred miles from their home-town in Yorkshire. I had joined them for the last few miles, aware that they had much greater stamina, but also blisters and aching knees – and a surge of energy with tears of joy as they stepped off the ferry.

This time they came by car, bringing another friend, Ros, whose journey began in Nigeria, and her carer, Chinonso – a stranger to us who became a friend. These two had never visited the island. With Ros now in a wheelchair, this visit moved at a different pace. Things which were famil-iar to some of us were seen in a new light through the questions of our companions. From a wheelchair landmarks are seen from a different angle, literally. It was humbling to learn through experience which places were accessible and which not. The statue of the Fallen Christ took on a deeper significance when Ros said that falling again and again was, strangely, helping her to journey with God.

For once, there were no long walks over hills or along beaches. Instead we accompanied each other on little expeditions – a stiff push up the brae, a bumpy crossing of grass, a circuit of the cloisters. But in our conversation we ranged through worlds of experience and years spent apart, recalling friends in many places. We shared worship and delight at the way it was a coming-home for some of us, a new-found land for others. Over meals, we talked about the faith that sustains us, our yearning for justice and the way that each of us works for it – connecting sustainable lifestyles and community development in West Yorkshire and Nigeria; caring for the marginalised – those living with leprosy, with mental illness – and learning from them; witnessing injustice in Israel/Palestine while accompanying those who challenge it. Out of our engagement welled up stories; out of our urgent desire for change, tears and laughter. This kind of encounter – the faith that folk bring with them – is one of the things that makes Iona holy ground.

Loving God, when we fall your wounded hands lift us up:
you give us companions on a journey, where strangers become friends;
you set our feet on holy ground, where justice and peace embrace –
we give you thanks, wholeheartedly. Amen

December 15: A highway … a causeway

Let the wilderness and the parched land be glad … let it rejoice and shout for joy … and a causeway shall appear there … it will become a pilgrim's way. (Isaiah 35:1,2, 8)

A year and a half after that time on Mull when I was stuck in the mud, I found myself far from home, in a dry land. The Australian outback was an alien, powerfully biblical landscape; but the humour of a bus driver was very down to earth. I found myself standing on red earth again, aware of a little family – God's children in that place.

Feet on the ground (2)

It was red earth, red as Adam,
a red sand-hill at the roadside;
and it tugged at my feet as I scrambled up.

Halfway down a highway
from nowhere to nowhere
was a rest-stop, with one beat-up pick-up parked.
The bus driver said, 'Check out the long-drop over there,
or, to grab a picture of Mount Conner –
and a salt lake into the bargain –
cross the road with care and climb up there.
Five minutes – we won't wait!'

Bus travel's sedentary:
the sand-hill was hard work.
Mount Conner loomed like a coal freighter

across miles of mulga scrub.
Nearer, the salt lake glittered.
But nearer still, on that little hill,
the family from the pick-up: kids larking about,
Father pointing out the view,
Mother, in a flowered dress,
taking pictures with her mobile phone.

That was what I came here to see –
not a view, but a family
who belonged on this long road,
and in this landscape, as I never could –
though my feet were red with dust.

God-with-us,
remind us that we human beings are made of the same red dust,
with your life breathed into us; that while we belong to different places,
we also belong together – and to you, as your loved children. Amen

December 16: Wildflower wander

Consider how the lilies grow in the fields; they do not work, they do not spin; yet I tell you, even Solomon in all his splendour was not attired like one of these. (Matthew 6:28,29)

Remember those golden days of midsummer? Here's one: In warm sunshine, a small group of people is walking out of the village in Iona, pausing to look into the hay meadows – not to spot the elusive corncrake, but to see how many species of wildflowers are there. We continue slowly along the road, stepping back to let tractors and bikes pass, pausing again and again to gaze into the grass of the verge. Flag irises, silverweed, clover, self-heal, shepherd's purse, speedwell, cranesbill, hawks-bit, bird's-foot trefoil, lady's bedstraw, orchids – yes and dandelions and thistles, buttercups and daisies too. What would be weeds elsewhere are being considered with delight. Scrambling down onto the shore, we see the silverweed colonising the sand, clumps of sea-rocket, and the thrift that thrives on saltings and inhospitable rocks.

This is a 'wildflower wander' led by Joyce, who lives here, loves and studies the flowers, and Emily, a National Trust Ranger. They point out plants, we ask questions, sometimes members of the group spot something first. Plant names are called out, and repeated with relish. Iona is an island where you can stride out enjoying beautiful landscapes, seascapes, skies coloured by dawn and sunset. But there is a special blessing in walking slowly, pausing often, looking carefully and intently at very small things, valuing them – for they are also God's handiwork.

In Jesus' three years of ministry there may not have been much time for wildflower wandering, but as he walked the tracks of the Galilee and the hill country, and through the fields and olive groves, he saw children playing and birds feeding on grain, farmers going about their work and weeds growing among the crops. He drew the attention of his disciples to the beauty of wildflowers – a sign of God's generous creativity. His 'lilies' were the scarlet anemones that spring up on the hillsides, at the roadsides, after the spring rains. Small things, exquisite but short-lived, reminding us of our mortality, and our value in God's eyes.

God of little things which are easily overlooked and don't last long,
help us to see that they – and we – are beautiful in your sight,
that every moment is precious. Amen

December 17: Through the borderlands

In the course of his journey to Jerusalem, Jesus was travelling through the borderlands of Samaria and Galilee. (Luke 17:11)

Jesus and his disciples would have been travelling on foot, giving plenty of time for conversations on the road, and face-to-face meetings with soldiers, critics, carers and outcasts. Followers of Jesus often find that walking with others helps us understand each other, which is part of finding God's way. As volunteers with EAPPI, we wore jackets with a distinctive logo combining a cross, barbed wire and a dove for peace, and we walked miles on dusty roads in the 'borderlands' where the West Bank meets Israel, accompanying Palestinian farmers and Israeli peace activists. Sometimes we had to stand still, to watch, so that we could bear witness. And sometimes we caught a bus!

Today

Today I saw a soldier in a prayer shawl,
with gun and phylactery and book,
bowing behind the humvee, beside the barbed wire
of the Separation Barrier: for him, maybe
as good – or bad – as any other place to pray,
today.

Today I travelled on a bus
where every passenger (coming tired from work)
greeted the driver and each other with
'Peace be upon you – and upon you, peace';
while the driver, who played *dabka* music all the way,

noticed the dove and cross on my vest
and wouldn't let me pay –
today.

God of peace and justice,
we pray for a change of heart
in those who believe that peace can be enforced by guns
and those who build barriers in fear;
we give thanks
for those
who live, day by day, in ways that make peace real.

December 18: Stand fast

Stand fast, I say. Fasten on the belt of truth; for a breastplate put on integrity; let the shoes on your feet be the gospel of peace, to give you firm footing; and with all these, take up the great shield of faith … (Ephesians 6:14–16)

Reading these words, I think of Gordon, a good friend whose life's journey has been coming to an end as I worked on this book. A good end to a good life – one of integrity and faith.

This book was inspired by many different people whose journeys I've shared for a little way – and who have encouraged me on mine. Pilgrims and Palestinian farmers, expectant mothers, dancing children and their protective grandparents, pacifists and activists, gardeners, knitters – bus drivers too.

Gordon, rather more conventionally, was a minister of the United Free Church. For many years his pastoral care and preaching were appreciated by different congregations. Then, approaching retirement, he and his wife, Nancy, felt that God was calling them to something different. They came to work for the Iona Community: Nancy as cook in the Abbey kitchen and Gordon as Sacristan ('beadle') in the Abbey Church. They were great colleagues. I was moved by the way that Gordon set aside the expected role of an ordained minister – who can be a solo player, speaking 'above contradiction' from the pulpit. He concentrated on being part of a team, and supporting those for whom leading worship was a new challenge. He and Nancy never compromised their principles, and spoke the truth in love to those with whom they disagreed, but they were not judgemental. Gordon's sense of humour leavened our common life: he enjoyed the paradox of introducing himself and his job to guests as 'a Free Church minister who enjoys liturgical worship, ringing bells and lighting candles'.

Soon after completing his contract in Iona, Gordon was discovered to have soft tissue sarcoma, and for the next few years lived with tests, treatment and then amputation. He lived as fully as possible, positively, gathering family, in touch with friends, and (when he could no longer be active) following the sporting events in which he delighted. In the face of pain and an uncertain future, he has lived as a whole person.

His is a story of healing – not about cure but about courage and God's transforming power. When the Commonwealth Games came to Glasgow, there he was, out on the streets, out of his wheelchair, in a kilt, balancing on his crutches and proudly holding aloft the baton. He stood firm; the shoes on his feet were the gospel of peace, as real as something the photographs couldn't quite show: the 'great shield of faith'.

O God, give us your shielding,
O God, give us your holiness,
O God, give us your comfort,
and your peace at our hour of death.

(Prayer from the Gaelic, in Iona Abbey Worship Book*)*

December 19: Watchful waiting

There was at that time in Jerusalem a man called Simeon ... who watched and waited ...' (Luke 2:25)

As the Gospels, in their different ways, describe events around the birth of Jesus, we become aware of many people watching and waiting. There are the two pregnant women, Elizabeth and Mary, of course. And the fathers-to-be: Zechariah, speechless at the news and waiting for the birth of a child in whom he could barely believe; Joseph, confused and then putting the whole matter into God's hands. There are the shepherds out in the fields, watching over their sheep, the Magi scanning the skies, Mary, reflecting on strange visitors with messages about angels, waiting to see what would happen next. And in Luke's Gospel, there in Jerusalem, the old man Simeon and the old woman Anna are waiting in the Temple for a baby to be brought for blessing, a child to be put into their arms.

A friend, John, who has just had a serious operation, says that the consultant encouraged him about his recovery, explained the tests that would need to follow, and said: 'You can get on with your life, while this is a time of watchful waiting.' For those of us getting older, this becomes a common experience – a discipline, a different time of grace. Here are words I wrote for Walt and Libby, friends who live far away now, from whom I have learned much:

Springtime in autumn

Among the kind green hills of Marin County,
springtime and autumn walk hand in hand.

The dogwood is blossoming at your door; by the window
small birds are busy about their nest ... you look out with love
at the life of your community through a garland of new leaves.
Yet you are both in your autumn now, aware of endings,
things falling away, the death of friends,
journeys that may never be made.
Is springtime in autumn a contradiction? Not when
there are such deep roots, such steadfast life, so much laughter.
There is no contradiction when – knowing how time is passing
and precious in our own lives – we look outwards,
dazzled and joyful, at the *kairos* of another dawn.

God, give us grace to wait; not to grieve over the passing of time,
but to greet with joy your coming, your transforming time. Amen

December 20: Under the tree

On either side of the river stood a tree of life, which yields twelve crops of fruit, one for each month of the year. The leaves of the trees are for the healing of the nations. (Revelation 22:2)

Many homes will already have a tree (real or artificial) in place, and presents being placed under the tree. One Advent, when I was an Ecumenical Accompanier in the West Bank Palestinian territories, the daily routine of our little international team – a fragile 'protective presence' for a hard-pressed village community – included accompanying farmers to their olive groves. Some of the trees were hundreds of years old. They were lovingly tended, like family members; their shade was welcome, their fruit and oil a source of livelihood and health, their presence in the land, sign of a God who provides for the needs of the people.

Soon after returning from the West Bank, I travelled in a bus along Oxford Street – it could have been any city centre in the run-up to Christmas. Garish artificial Christmas trees contrasted with the reality of the olive groves in the lives of people in the Holy Land – their down-to-earth usefulness and deep symbolism.

Under this unreal tree,
with fluorescent greenery –
can hope be born?

Among glittering promises,
deadlines, expectations –
will hope be born?

Among full fridges and diaries,
with empty words –
can hope be born?
Through tough reality,
in the dark, in quiet expectancy –
hope is born.

Under the olive tree,
in our common humanity –
hope is born.

Living, loving, growing God, help us to grasp your reality
and to see hope being born in hard places
and where people have lost heart. Amen

December 21: Weeping for her children

A voice was heard in Rama, sobbing in bitter grief; it was Rachel weeping for her children, and refusing to be comforted, because they were no more. (Matthew 2:18)

This is still Advent, a time of waiting, of expectancy, of the potential for great joy – and also a time of risk and forebodings. Will the time to which we look forward be a day of judgement, a day when the sky will grow dark? In Matthew's Gospel the star-led Magi have already begun their journey, which will lead them to Herod's palace, where their innocent questions will stir up his wrath.

Ecumenical Accompaniers, who work and walk alongside Palestinian and Israeli peace activists on the West Bank for three months, also travel together into Israel, to encounter a different society, a different perspective, to ask questions too. But, because of the blockade, we could not go into Gaza. I have only travelled as far as the border of this open-air prison camp, home to human beings who, as anywhere else, can be both kindly and cruel, creative and frustrated, joyful and fearful. As I write this their fear must be overwhelming, with war planes once more overhead and tanks on the streets. People – made in the image of God – are suffering terrible violence. So many children are dying. This is the massacre of the innocents.

The nearest I've come to Gaza (in a time of relative peace) is to the edge of an Israeli kibbutz; with the folk we met there we looked toward their neighbours' home: But, because of the blockade, we could not cross into Gaza.

A glimpse of Gaza

Beyond intensively green fields – a land cultivated for all its worth
(we have ways of making the desert bloom) –
and past barbed wire and thorny scrub,
beyond low sandy hills are pale buildings out of focus,
a complicated cluster of communication masts:
ragged edges of a city in the heat haze,
like a dream on the edge of waking –
dislocated – a different reality getting lost in the hard light of day,
beyond belief: but this is where people live and love and grieve.
Dust, poppies, a sound of distant gunfire … beyond, the sea.
Yes, this is Gaza, no mistaking: tears blur, words fail. Gaze.

God of compassion, we gaze at newspaper or television screen.
We cannot comprehend such grief.
That woman with her dead child carries the weight of the world.
Yet you are there: you did not turn away,
you share her pain. Amen

December 22: Called by name

Can a woman forget the infant at her breast, or a mother the child of her womb? But should even these forget, I shall never forget you. I have inscribed you on the palms of my hands. (Isaiah 49:14–16a)

Every child is a child of God. Each one of us is precious to God. I wondered, when I began this book, whether it would be helpful to you who are using these reflections to read the real names of those whose journeys I have shared, to whom I owe such gratitude for the way they have accompanied me. Would so many names be confusing, I wondered, or leave the reader feeling excluded? And yet it felt important that at some point I used their given name, the one by which family and friends know them, the name that is 'written on God's palm', cradling each one of us.

Visiting Yad Vashem, the Holocaust Museum in Jerusalem, is an overwhelming experience. The shocking lessons of history confront us, and – without denying them – it is possible to hear strong political points being made for the present. The experience is most moving when the dead are honoured: In a huge darkened hall, tiny points of light appear briefly as different voices speak the names, one by one, of men, women, children who died in the concentration camps. Each one a child of God. Each of these human beings was/is known and loved by God: the message of Psalm 139, to which these reflections have returned again and again.

As I worked on this book the people in Gaza were suffering appalling violence (as happened in many other places the same year – Syria, Sudan, the Central African Republic – places that blink on the edge of our vision briefly). Listening from far off, we feel helpless. How can we even pray, in the face of such huge suffering? The website of B'Tselem, an Israeli organisation dedicated to working for a just peace and monitoring the effects of the Occupation, ran a constant update of pictures of the onslaught on Gaza, with statistics. And also, across the top of the page, a succession of names of children who had been killed: their family names, their given names. Each of these a child of God. Each of these was/is known and loved by God.

While we went on campaigning and working for a just peace, we were enabled to pray for these children by name – as members of the same human family, for whom the words of God according to the prophet also ring true: *Have no fear, for I have redeemed you; I call you by name; you are mine.* (Isaiah 43:1b)

December 23: Advent expectancy

Though you will be plunged in grief, your grief will be turned to joy. A woman in labour is in pain because her time has come; but when her baby is born she forgets the anguish in her joy that a child has been born into the world. (John 16:20b–21)

Before the strong sensations of childbirth comes a long time of waiting – with many different sensations and mixed feelings, including both apprehension and hope. Our culture, hearsay and human nature create particular expectations. Some are more realistic than others. The same can be true of folk on a journey of faith. Rigid expectations can be disappointed. But expectancy, openness to good things that may happen (though we cannot control them) – to God mysteriously at work – that can help us face the unknown.

A couple of years ago, both my daughters, Anna and Meg, were pregnant, expecting their first babies in the New Year. Living in our modern world, they and their partners, Bobbie and Paul, had access to all kinds of information, from scans and blood tests. They were attending preparation classes and had already made choices (unlike Mary and Joseph) about where and how they would like to give birth. But there was still the huge uncertainty of the actual event. Expectations could only take them so far on the journey. So Advent was indeed, for our family, a time of expectancy.

This was my Advent reflection for that time:

Walking
in darkness,
learning a new dance,
growing under the earth,
swimming in a midnight sea

wakeful, watchful, wonderful,
shocking, surprising, setting free

coming closer:
changing you, me
– everything –
becoming,
giving birth.

The above was written before, with tears of joy, our family welcomed first Linus, then Erin into the world. Now we enjoy their presence, as part of our family. Advent is a reminder of the waiting time. Now, looking for a sign of God-with-us, the world holds its breath.

We longed and waited:
now the contractions have started:
Midwife God, deliver us. Amen

December 24: Christmas Eve in the city

Surely darkness is not too dark for you and night is as light as day; to you both dark and light are one ... You know me through and through; my body was no mystery to you, when I was formed in secret, woven in the depths of the earth ... my life was fashioned before it had come into being ... Examine me and know my mind; test me and understand my anxious thoughts. Watch lest I follow any path that grieves you; lead me in the everlasting way. (Psalm 139:11–12,14–16,23–24)

I was 33, living in a rough part of Inner London, a mile from the church where a midnight service was held on Christmas Eve; I had baked bread for Communion. Late at night I carried it to the church, through rowdy streets. I was also carrying a child in my womb, fearful about the future of the world into which that child would be born. Conflict and uncertainty cast shadows on the happiness of our family, shaking my confidence. Yet I was also filled with joyful hope for that new life. The bread was my reason for that difficult journey, and that night I felt God walking with me.

Communion bread

Carrying this bread through the midnight city, I am a passer-by,
stepping over the broken glass, uneven pavements, the dark puddles;
past houses curtained, shrugging off the street, screen-lit;
past hoardings with their obscenities and philosophies,
sidestepping clinches and wrangles –
blows struck in a confusion of feelings;
past empty houses and empty faces, under the motorway –
lights travelling from nowhere to nowhere.

Midway between conception and birth, carrying this bread, newly baked;
I bear a secret more enduring than the city:
a fragrance against the petrol fumes,
a growing thing to rock these barren towers,
and heal the self-destruction of these streets.
I carry this bread to be shared among waiting people in the still church.
Carrying this bread, I'm caught up in living patterns of the city.
Not just a passer-by, but becoming part in what I fear,
what links me to others.
The bread I bear now, the child I will bear in the uncertain future –
because of these, I am threatened.
Yet I walk safely through the midnight streets,
carrying something more than myself – the weight of a world.

Loving God, who in Jesus was born as one of us –
a helpless baby in a dangerous world –
be with those who are homeless, powerless, afraid tonight,
with those who hunger for bread and for love;
and with those who have bread to share – in your name and for your sake.
Walk with us, and be present in the breaking of bread. Amen

To LOVE MERCY
Act JUSTLY
and WALK
HUMBLY
with YOUR GOD

Sources and acknowledgements

Bible passages from Revised English Bible (except the paraphrases of verses from Psalms 23 and 85, and the version of Micah 6:8 in Steve Raw's cover artwork). Scripture quotations taken from the Revised English Bible, copyright © Cambridge University Press and Oxford University Press 1989. All rights reserved.

Wild Goose Publications is part of the Iona Community:

- An ecumenical movement of men and women from different walks of life and different traditions in the Christian church
- Committed to the gospel of Jesus Christ, and to following where that leads, even into the unknown
- Engaged together, and with people of goodwill across the world, in acting, reflecting and praying for justice, peace and the integrity of creation
- Convinced that the inclusive community we seek must be embodied in the community we practise

Together with our staff, we are responsible for:

- Our islands residential centres of Iona Abbey, the MacLeod Centre on Iona, and Camas Adventure Centre on the Ross of Mull

and in Glasgow:

- The administration of the Community
- Our work with young people
- Our publishing house, Wild Goose Publications
- Our association in the revitalising of worship with the Wild Goose Resource Group

The Iona Community was founded in Glasgow in 1938 by George MacLeod, minister, visionary and prophetic witness for peace, in the context of the poverty and despair of the Depression. Its original task of rebuilding the monastic ruins of Iona Abbey became a sign of hopeful rebuilding of community in Scotland and beyond. Today, we are about 250 Members, mostly in Britain, and 1500 Associate Members, with 1400 Friends worldwide. Together and apart, 'we follow the light we have, and pray for more light'.

For information on the Iona Community contact:
The Iona Community, Fourth Floor, Savoy House, 140 Sauchiehall Street,
Glasgow G2 3DH, UK. Phone: 0141 332 6343
e-mail: admin@iona.org.uk; web: www.iona.org.uk

For enquiries about visiting Iona, please contact:
Iona Abbey, Isle of Iona, Argyll PA76 6SN, UK. Phone: 01681 700404
e-mail: ionacomm@iona.org.uk